THE SECRET DIARY OF A LAWYER

THE SECRET DIARY OF A LAWYER

How to survive and thrive in a City law firm

BELLE DE JURE

Copyright © 2023 by Belle de Jure

All rights reserved. No part of this book may be reproduced or used in any manner without written permission of the copyright owner except for the use of quotations in a book review.

FIRST EDITION

ISBNs
Paperback: 978-1-80227-848-4
eBook: 978-1-80541-088-1

Contents

Preface vii

Part I: The Newbie

Chapter 1   The made-up task 3
Chapter 2   Marathon not a race 9
Chapter 3   The difficult PA 15
Chapter 4   The mobile phone 19

Part II: Catching on

Chapter 5   Do you have capacity? 27
Chapter 6   How do you solve a problem like Maria? 31
Chapter 7   All work and no lunch 37
Chapter 8   Great Expectations 41

Part III: Old Hand

Chapter 9   I'm all yours 49
Chapter 10 How to sleep with the lights on 55
Chapter 11 Rules of engagement 63
Chapter 12 Pro-bono 69

Part IV: The Flipside

Chapter 13 Embrace the unknown 77
Chapter 14 Make sure the shoe fits 83
Chapter 15 No frills 87
Chapter 16 The grass looks greener 95

Preface

When I found out that I had landed a training contract at a prestigious Magic Circle law firm in London, I was thrilled. All my hard work had finally paid off and I couldn't wait to embark on my career as a high-flying lawyer in the City. I was ready to learn from the best and become the best.

I was nervous though. I knew it wouldn't be easy and I decided to keep a diary. Something I could look back on years later.

This book is a collection of stories from my diary (modified slightly, of course, to protect my identity). Before you ask, yes, I have had a very successful career. I enjoyed my time at said Magic Circle firm, did very well, and, if you ask me whether I would do it all again, I'd say yes, absolutely.

But there are a number of things I had to figure out for myself. Tips and tricks I wish I had known earlier. Each story has a moral at the end, capturing what I learned from the event.

I hope you enjoy this book. The stories are all true so if you are setting out on your journey, I hope you learn something that prepares you for what lies ahead. If you are already on your journey, I hope you can relate and laugh along!

Enjoy my diary!

PART I

The Newbie

CHAPTER 1

The made-up task

Induction over, I arrived at my office raring to go. Having been warned not to wear a black suit[1], I had on a smart white blouse and grey pencil skirt. I was dressed to impress. It was 9 a.m. and my supervisor was already at his desk, no doubt typing out a complex financing agreement that was worth millions.

He looked up and smiled as I walked in. "That's a good sign", I thought to myself. You hear a lot of horror stories in the world of City law firms. Stories of supervisors of all shapes, sizes and characters.

There were the dark, Snape-like personalities. Seemingly malevolent and always out to trip up newbies.

Then you have the Gollums. Other-worldly creatures from an altogether different fairy-tale. To them, every sentence is a puzzle. Every word both delights and tortures them. Preferring the windowless offices in the bowels of the firm, they shy away from the world. Such an individual often becomes obsessed and paranoid, consumed by work and fascinated by the very object that slowly sucks the life out of them.

---

[1] I was told black was for the rookie, still clinging to his past life as a waiter paying off his student loan.

Then there are the old bespectacled Dumbledores - a dying breed. Founts of knowledge, but so out of touch with technology that their trainees' only task is to teach and re-teach them how to turn on the computers. Later on, I was to learn that one of my colleagues had the misfortune of sitting with one particularly old old-timer who mistrusted the use of automatic numbering on documents. This trainee often burned the midnight oil as every time an amendment was made, his task was to manually renumber the clauses on documents, which often ran to hundreds of pages. Another trainee was constantly told off for failing to write the date and time at the top of every email. His attempts to explain that the creators of Outlook had thought of this were dismissed as improbable.

My supervisor looked pleasant enough (and appeared competent on the computer) so I heaved a sigh of relief and took a seat. We exchanged pleasantries, and, after I had settled down, my supervisor cleared his throat and said, "I have a task for you". The sensation I felt in my stomach was one of general discomfort; that sensation you get just before an exam. I told myself (in my head) that I was ready, I was prepared and yet I knew that so much depended on my performance of this task, whatever it was. Voices in my head whispered, "First impressions are vital", "Mess this up and you will be banished to the document review room where you will have to spend the next six months trawling through badly organised, decaying stacks of documents".

I put on my best smile and said, "Happy to help".

The made-up task

My supervisor smiled back and said, "I don't have that much on at the moment that you could help with, but it would be really helpful if you could print out a copy of Mervyn King's latest speech and the appendix".

And then came a question - a simple question - one that I knew the answer to and one that would haunt me for the next six months. "Do you know who Mervyn King is?" Of course, I did. I had even attended a speech he delivered at my university, but, at that moment, my mind went blank. I had that sick, dizzy feeling you get on a plane when there is too much turbulence. This is a feeling I was to become accustomed to during my time at the firm.

I didn't say anything but simply moved my head in a motion that was somewhere between a nod and a shake. This too was a defensive action that I would become accustomed to using during my time at the firm. My supervisor looked slightly perplexed, then his face relaxed and he muttered something like, "Ok, good, then get on with it". I too relaxed and, in that moment, I remembered who Mervyn King[2] was. I spun around in my chair but it was too late.

These law firms pride themselves on commercial awareness – knowing their clients, understanding the markets and knowing the big players and influencers. My supervisor was typing away no doubt contemplating his misfortune at being allocated such an 'un-commercial' trainee.

---

[2] Just for the record, Mervyn King was the Governor of the Bank of England at the time.

I decided that I had to redeem myself. I had to find the speech and print it out extra fast. I would also staple it, no, I would put it in a plastic folder, no, a ring binder with a clear label. A few searches run on Google, a few clicks of my mouse and I had the speech in front of me. Now, if only I could remember how to use the big colour printer. Ah yes, I managed to figure it out without assistance from the particularly moody secretary I had been allocated. My months of work experience were paying off. In a few minutes, I could hear the speech printing off. Not wanting to leave anything to chance, I walked over to the printer and waited until my printing was finished. I collected the pages, hole-punched them neatly, put them in a ring binder, which I labelled, and then presented it proudly to my supervisor.

"Thanks," my supervisor said as he took the binder from me, "but it appears that there's a bit missing. The printer sometimes runs out of paper; it's not your fault". I felt faint. How could I be so foolish? Why hadn't I checked?

My supervisor didn't ask me to do anything else that day and, as I walked home that evening, I felt awful.

Moral of the story: Always check the printer has enough paper? Well, yes, but there was more to it than that. The binder containing the speech (fully printed, appendix and all) sat on my supervisor's shelf for months, unread and untouched. This had clearly been a made-up task, but I learned a lot about the nature of lawyers from it:

1) Lawyers by default mistrust the competence of others. Why else check the number of pages, especially if he wasn't even going to read the speech?

The made-up task

2) As I spent more time at the firm, I became accustomed to being challenged, but I also learned that everyone (including the Magic Circle elite) makes mistakes. Don't sweat the small stuff. If you make a mistake, rectify it if you can, and move on.

3) Always check that the printer has enough paper.

Chapter 2

Marathon not a race

I recall my first two weeks at the firm. Trainee induction consisted of a series of daily lectures and presentations starting at 9 a.m. and finishing at 5.30 p.m. By the end of my first day, my brain was fried, my back ached and I longed to get out of the uncomfortable clothes I was wearing.

I had met many of the people in my intake on the Legal Practice Course and they were a friendly enough bunch, but, as the day dragged on, I just wanted to go home and relax on my own. As the clock ticked by, I could visualise a hot bath, the television on and a takeaway pizza.

5.30 p.m. finally came and we were told that we were free to leave. The school bell sounding the end of the day was ringing out gloriously and then... up shot a hand. "Excuse me," one of my fellow trainees said, "I assume we can now go up to our offices to see if there is something we can help our supervisors with?"

The course conductor smiled and replied, "Yes, for those of you who wish to do so, please feel free to pop up and say hello". My heart sank as several of my new friends began to make their way towards the elevators and then up to their respective offices.

I was sure my supervisor was not expecting to see me that evening and I could not bear the thought of another hour or two at work so, after much deliberation, I slipped out.

As soon as I walked out the door, a gust of cold wind hit me and I felt invigorated. I inhaled deeply and smiled. The euphoric moment was, however, not to last. As I walked home and for the rest of that evening, I started second-guessing myself. Should I have stayed? What if my supervisor saw the other first-seat trainees back from induction and thought I was playing hooky?

The next morning, I was keen to find out what the others had gotten up to in their offices. We sat down in our designated seats and I leaned over to get myself a glass of water, moving my name card on the table ever so slightly so that my name was no longer an easy target for presenters who liked contributions from the floor. This was a trick I had learned the day before.

As I poured myself a glass, I asked the girl next to me, "So, did you go and see your supervisor yesterday?" "No", she replied. "He was in a meeting, so I decided to go home." I felt a little relieved.

As I looked around the room, I noticed that several people I had seen the day before had not yet arrived. I might have put it down to lateness but then these particular individuals tended to be at least 15 minutes early for everything. Had they decided they had had enough after just one day? Perhaps they were ill… but all of them?

The first presentation started and, 20 minutes later, the four missing trainees turned up. They looked unusually unkempt, red-eyed and very apologetic. I later learned why.

Eger, one of the four vagabonds, explained excitedly over lunch that upon heading up to his office the previous night, he had met his supervisor, Mark. Mark seemed nice enough and thanked Eger for his offer of assistance but said he should go home as Mark had not been expecting him that day. Eger left the room, passing the large glass windows of other offices. Suddenly, a tall broad figure called out, "You!" Eger spun around and was confronted by the chest of the towering senior partner, nicknamed the "Terminator".

The Terminator repeated, "You, boy, where are you going?" "I came to ask if I could assist with anything and am on my way home," Eger stuttered. "You can assist me," the Terminator spat, pointing to a room across the corridor. "Go in there and report to… the chap with the glasses." Then he was gone.

Poor Eger; he spent the rest of the night trawling through hundreds of badly printed documents that had been piled into mouldy boxes. Our client had obviously buried their legal contracts in the basement and they had now been unearthed from their dank graves in preparation for the transaction. Eger was to be on the lookout for the elusive "change of control clause". Twelve hours playing hide-and-seek and he had managed to find one. Jubilant, the red-eyed trainee scurried off to the associate in charge pointing at the faint text on one of the documents. The associate inspected the text, nodded and said to come back when he had found at least ten more.

I was mortified when I heard the story. Eger, however, had a smile on his face. If that was the kind of work they were handing out, I wasn't sure I wanted it. Don't get me wrong; I knew what I had signed up for but the reality of the drudgery ahead hit home. Had I made the wrong choice coming here?

Eger spent the next few evenings up on the seventh floor, reviewing uninteresting documents. He boasted about how many 'all-nighters' he had done and how much more than us he was learning. Yeah, right.

I was to meet many Egers during my time at the firm. 'Eager beavers' we called them, already planning their path to partnership. I was therefore surprised to learn that Eger lasted only a couple of years, quitting as soon as he qualified.

Once induction had finally come to an end, and Eger had spent his second weekend at work, he walked into his office on Monday morning. He looked tired and a little dishevelled but, being Eger, was excited to get started. His supervisor Mark was not impressed to learn that Eger had been assigned more document review by the Terminator and told him that he would need to do that in the evenings, concentrating on tasks that Mark required assistance with during the day. Eger was a classic 'burn out' case. He continued to try his best but, being only human, simply became more and more tired and disillusioned until one day he cracked.

Moral of the story:

1) As a rule, I rarely went in search of work - don't worry, it will always find you.

2) Eger made the mistake of being caught loitering. Don't loiter - only senior partners are allowed to do that.
3) Most importantly, working at a law firm is a marathon, not a race, so pace yourself.

You might think to yourself after reading this book that I was a shirker. Let me tell you, I had my fair share of all-nighters. The difference I suppose was that most of my all-nighters were not at some senior partner's whim. I stayed because there was no other option and a deal was close to being done. Remember, we are all only human and there is only so much you are physically capable of. Also, life must go on outside of work, so don't let work become all-consuming.

CHAPTER **3**

The difficult PA

Personal Assistants at law firms wield more power than you would imagine and, just as you have partners with varying personalities, the same is true of secretaries.

The old guard- PAs who started at the firm before I was born and who know it like the back of their hand.

Positives and negatives: The old guard tend to be like loyal dogs – totally loyal to the partner they have been working for, know their masters' habits and can judge their moods like no one else but have difficulty learning any new tricks (especially where technology is concerned). They like to go for long walks in the afternoon, have plenty of treats (especially at Christmas time) and generally do little actual work. They can, however, read some pretty illegible handwriting, are caring and understanding and will mother you on difficult days.

The twenty-something novices. Positives: usually whizzes with technology and always eager to please. Negatives: sometimes more eager to please those of the male gender.

Then you have the middle-aged PAs. Their personalities are a mixed bag. I had the misfortune of having a particularly salty woman in her late thirties in my first seat as a trainee. Let's call her Briny.

Briny constantly complained of aches and pains, huffing and puffing whenever I dared to ask her to do something. She had the ability to make me feel insignificant and silly. Briny was, however, very efficient and, on the rare occasion that she agreed to do something for me, she usually did it very well.

The most difficult aspect of my relationship with Briny was that my supervisor adored her. Of course, she behaved very differently with my supervisor. Giving Briny a task was like playing with a boomerang - it always ended up back on my desk (with some delay), making me seem incompetent. Peering over my shoulder at my screen in the evenings, my supervisor would sometimes tut and say, "You should have just given it to Briny as I suggested. That is really a job for a PA".

What could I say in response? "Briny won't listen to me"? I would have sounded like a petulant child in kindergarten, so I kept silent.

It was on one fateful day that my supervisor came to realise what Briny was up to. Briny had been assigned to Terry (a fourth-seat trainee) for a week as his PA was ill. Terry was much more worldly than I was, having spent a year and a half more at the firm than me. It only took a day and Terry, who didn't have the same reverence for supervisors that I did, waltzed into my room and declared, "Man, your secretary is crazy".

My supervisor looked up but didn't say anything as the comment hadn't been directed at him. I looked apologetically at my supervisor for the interruption. Terry, ignoring my pleading look to shut up, continued, "She is meant to be helping me today. I saw her on Amazon a few times and she insists she can't do anything for me as she is too busy. "I pity you being stuck with her".

Not waiting for a response, he turned and walked out. I didn't know what to do and in my flustered state, I stared straight ahead at my screen trying unsuccessfully to pretend I hadn't seen or heard Terry.

My supervisor cleared his throat and said, "Have you had any problems with Briny?" How to respond? I didn't want to get Briny in trouble.

I said, "Well, she is very good... when she has the time to help me. She seems very busy usually though". Nothing more was said, but I found Briny changed after that. She became more willing to help me. Now, I'm not sure whether this was because of something my supervisor said or whether she realised that I wasn't so bad after her encounter with Terry.

Tips if you encounter a Briny:

1) Don't let her smell fear. Be polite and courteous but never doubt yourself.
2) You will come across a variety of personalities. Remember that they will all have strengths and weaknesses and some are better suited to certain tasks than others.

Chapter 4

The mobile phone

As humans, we tend to fear the unknown. The best horror movies make full use of the powers of suggestion, subtly planting the seeds of terror which, nourished by our imagination, sprout into our own worst fears.

When I started as a trainee, I was in a world where BlackBerrys, rather than iPhones, were the norm. For those who don't know, Blackberrys had a little flashing devil light. Every time you got an email, the red light would flash and the Eye of Sauron would demand your immediate attention.

I had to wait a few weeks before my work phone was set up and ready to collect. I had been warned that having a BlackBerry meant surrendering your freedom to the firm. No one can hide from the all-seeing Eye. You aren't safe anywhere. "It's like being chained to the office," I was warned. I awaited my fate in terror.

But, like most rumours that circulate the offices of the legal elite, these rumours proved to be false.

The days went on and I soon realised that the worst thing about working at a law firm is the unpredictability. Questions I asked myself almost daily were:

Should I try and go into work a bit early or can I afford another half an hour of sleep? If I sleep now, am I wasting valuable time that I could be spending on a task that is already sitting in my inbox? Is anything sitting in my inbox? Will my morning be busy or will I have to sit around twiddling my thumbs until something comes up? Will it be a late night and should I therefore try and get a bit more sleep?

Should I go for a quick walk in the afternoon and get some fresh air or will someone be looking for me?

Should I go to this training session? It looks interesting but what if the document I am expecting comes in? I may be here till midnight if I am not able to start on it immediately!

It is 8 p.m. and my supervisor is nowhere to be seen. Can I go home? Has he gone home or is he at dinner or in a meeting? What if he needs something?

Did I leave too early tonight? What if I wake up to 20 emails all marked urgent?

These questions plagued me; that is, until I got a BlackBerry. I realised that my fears about having a BlackBerry were unfounded. It was not an added burden. In fact, I found it was quite the opposite – it actually gave me my freedom.

No longer was I chained to my laptop – I felt I could come and go as I pleased as I would know immediately if there was something I should be doing. I could plan my day (and my sleep) better. I could stay for lunch in the canteen for longer and I could attend all the mildly useful training sessions without the fear that I would have to make up for lost time at midnight.

Having my BlackBerry removed the unknown from the equation.

The mobile phone

Now, I must warn you that not all people found the BlackBerry liberating. For some, the flashing red light of the BlackBerry was hypnotic. It held them in a spellbound alternative reality where only life at work existed and from which they could not escape into the real world. How do you avoid falling prey to such a fate? Here are my tips for you.

1) How often should I check my emails after I leave the office/after working hours?

   We live in a world of boundaries. Nations have boundaries, our homes have boundaries, and even dogs mark their territory. I think it is important to create your own 'work phone boundary'. You need to set a reasonable time every evening after which you will not look at your work mobile either because you turn your phone off or you put it in a corner for the night. If you decide to place it in a corner, I suggest the corner is not anywhere near your bed.

   This rule is more important than you think and you need to stick to it. If you respond to emails after your designated cut-off time, you create an expectation.

   I must admit that there were a few times I unexpectedly received an email at 11 p.m. with the expectation that I would still be awake, sober and ready to spring into action. People I was working with, however, soon realised and grew accustomed to the fact that I would not respond after my cut-off. For me, that was 7 p.m., unless we were in the midst of a transaction and an impending deadline loomed. On the occasions I needed to be up late, I was forewarned.

2) What about emails on the weekend? Do I have to respond?

No. Senior associates and partners sometimes send you emails over the weekend not because they are urgent but simply because they don't want to forget to tell you to do something. The same rule applies as above - unless you have specifically been forewarned to check your emails, switch your phone off. Don't reply. Don't create unhealthy expectations.

3) What about when I'm on holiday?

Unless you have been told that you will need to monitor emails, turn your phone off.

By the way, this may be a good time to briefly touch on holidays and out-of-office messages more generally.

Rule 1 – try to book long holidays rather than 2-3 days off. Partners are less likely to get someone to cover for you on a short holiday. This will mean that either you will have to work during your time away or you will have a cloud of work looming over your head when you return.

Rule 2 - My out-of-office message always simply read "I am out of the office between X and Y and will not have access to emails during this time. If your query is urgent, contact another member of my team". Don't volunteer "I will have intermittent access to emails" or (even worse) "I will try to check my emails regularly". Remember what I said about creating boundaries and expectations?

The only exceptions to the above rules are when you are on a deal that has reached the stage where it requires constant attention. In that case, you should have been told to monitor your emails anyway. And in my personal opinion, there's no point in wasting valuable holiday time then - try and postpone.

Moral of the story: Technology can set you free if you use it wisely. You do, however, need to set clear boundaries, both for yourself and others.

By the way, setting boundaries is more important than ever post-pandemic. If you're not careful, you can all too easily become trapped in a twilight zone between work and home life.

PART II

Catching on

Chapter 5

Do you have capacity?

These are four words that you will likely come to know and fear.

Fast forward to five years at the firm (can you believe it!) and what came to interest me was the array of reactions these four simple words would solicit. I found that you could class the reactions into roughly three types.

To put these words into a little more context, each week the trainees and associates in my group were subjected to the 'rounds'. This is when a partner, usually a more junior partner upon whom this arduous task had been dumped, goes around to each person's office and says, "Do you have capacity?" The partner then marks your response on a clipboard he carries around and all the partners have a big meeting the next morning to discuss each person's capacity and work allocation.

Coming back to the three types.

Type 1. Those who always say "yes". I had a friend at the firm, well, more of an acquaintance really. Let's call him Roger. Roger was your classic Type 1 case. He firmly believed that anything other than a "yes" would anger or annoy the partner on his rounds. As a result, work simply piled up on Roger. In fact, there were very few instances when I did not see Roger beavering away when I left the office. Roger, as you might imagine, was another burn-out.

Roger developed a reputation for being unreliable and, wait for it, lazy! Who would have thought?!

A funny story (not so funny for Roger) of his encounter with the Terminator demonstrates my case. The Terminator, as you will remember, is the towering senior partner who banished poor Eger to the dungeon of document review on his first day at the firm.

From a rather strapping trainee, Roger quickly developed a belly (probably from all the all-nighters sustained by consuming a mix of coffee, Diet Coke and pizza) and became a beady-eyed associate. The Christmas holidays came and went and Roger decided that his New Year's resolution was to make regular visits to the gym. One evening, as Roger was changing out of his gym clothes in the firm's locker room, getting ready for yet another late night at the office, he felt a foreboding presence behind him.

The Terminator, who took pride in his good figure and manly appearance, believed that his manhood should be flaunted in the men's locker room so that the weedy associates could aspire not only to his professional but also his physical accomplishments.

Roger, as you can imagine, was speechless and his eyes, quite involuntarily, scanned the great figure up and down. The figure towered over him, hands on his hips and a voice boomed, "So, board minutes. Where are they?" Roger was speechless for a while and then managed a meek "almost done". The figure of the Terminator boomed, "Then get to it, boy. What are you doing here?"

Type 2. Those who always say something like "maybe", "I will probably have some time tomorrow or Tuesday or next week," or "I am quite busy but I can try and make some time" or "Yes, as long as it does not take up too much time". You might think that this type of reply sounds like a sensible, more diplomatic response. It failed, however, to take into account a number of factors, leaving the subject as vulnerable as the person using the Type 1 response.

First, this type of response, while it sounds good when spoken, is rarely what gets written down on the partner's clipboard. The already stressed/fed-up partner doing the rounds rarely bothers writing down "perhaps, but only if it is a small task". A Type 2 subject usually simply gets a tick next to his or her name.

Second, partners always underestimate the amount of time a task will take. Don't forget that they have years of experience and while they may think a task is 'small', it may in fact take a more junior associate hours. Third, once you have been allocated a task, you are stuck with it. Partners are human. They too like to go home at a decent hour and once they have found a subject to take on a task, saying to them that you can only spend 2 hours on it is not an acceptable excuse.

Type 3. Those who very rarely say "yes". I started as a Type 2 and quickly realised that Type 3 is the more sensible category to be in. Now, you might think to yourself that this type comes across as unenthusiastic; lazy even. Or surely you can't use this approach and then leave at 6 p.m. while your colleagues are busy at work? I thought the same until I had the fortune of sitting with Frankie.

Frankie, my third-seat supervisor, really knew how to play the game. She was very good at her job, had the respect of all the partners in the group and yet frequently waltzed out of the office at 6 p.m. Not only that, but each time a partner came over to the office to do his rounds, Frankie simply said she could not take on any more work and that was that. It was accepted and the partner said "no problem" and walked away. I discovered a few things about this approach.

First, Frankie had enough time to do each task thoroughly. Unlike those in Types 1 and 2, Frankie was not overloaded or tired and, as a consequence, the partners came to respect her efficiency and thoroughness. Second, partners are generally not spiteful individuals who like to see people suffer long into the night. Frankie was respected for all the extracurricular activities she got up to and was often invited out to client entertainment events, being a generally more interesting person than the tired dishevelled weedy beavers.

Third, working at a law firm does not require you to win a popularity contest. There were some partners that Frankie never worked with. Individuals in Types 1 and 2 tended to aim to work with every partner in the group, but I soon learned that some partners are best avoided. Finally, with a Type 3, you always know where you stand. The answer to the question is always yes or no - never "maybe", "perhaps" or "next Monday", etc.

Moral of the story: Be a Frankie not a Roger.

Chapter 6

How do you solve a problem like Maria?

Maria was an interesting character. She was a relatively senior associate and I frequently asked myself how she had lasted this long - not at the firm but on the planet.

Maria was prone to fits of panic. She was your typical pessimistic glass-half-empty kind of person who mistrusted everyone around her. In fact, having worked extensively with her, I found that she frequently mistrusted herself.

She constantly complained to me about how much work she had on and how she was having to re-draft work produced by others.

Drafting is a subject with so many different views amongst lawyers. I am generally of the more liberal view, "if it ain't broke don't fix it". Maria, on the other hand, was a linguistic purist who was a serial re-drafter. Needless to say, her constant meddling did not make her popular with the lawyers on the other side nor, indeed, with her own colleagues.

From reading this book, you will learn that I tend to have more laid-back/liberal views on most issues – the unimportant ones anyway. I came to the realisation early on that you have to pick your battles carefully. Maria, on the other hand, fought for every point, re-wrote every piece of work anyone produced, insisted on being copied into every email no matter how insignificant, re-researched every research note and questioned everything. Maria and I were therefore diametrically opposite characters - recipe for disaster you might think.

Maria and I, together with another junior associate called Jack, were teamed up to work on a rather complex transaction. Each of us was given a workstream. Jack and I, being the juniors, were to report to Maria.

Jack was in the same trainee intake as me. He could be a tad serious sometimes but I liked him and he was good at his job.

We had our transaction "kick-off call"[3], which went smoothly and we each took away what I thought was a short and relatively simple task to get started on. Our client seemed very reasonable and mentioned that there was no rush with the tasks. I completed my task in about an hour and, as I had had an otherwise slow day, and given that it was already 6 p.m., I went home.

I checked my phone in the usual way just before dinner to see if there was anything urgent and I was surprised to see seven new emails. They were all from Maria, demanding an update on the status of our (non-urgent) tasks. I replied saying that I had completed my task and she could have a look at it the next day. Back shot an email, almost immediately, saying that she would prefer to look at it that evening.

---

[3] This is the first conversation you have with your client. They explain what they want and you explain how you can get them there.

I was to become very familiar with this late-night badgering and Jack and I were to have very different approaches to dealing with Maria.

The next morning, I had on my desk a copy of the document I had sent Maria the previous night, completely amended - red lettering all over the place. I was filled with a mixture of anger and disgust – we lawyers take pride in our work. I have a tendency to react impulsively and I marched over to Maria's office but she was gone. I then came back to my desk to read her track-changes and discovered that the document in front of me was simply re-worded. It was redrafted to conform with Maria's style but there was nothing new; no value added.

I marched over to Jack's office and found him red-faced, a can of Diet Coke in one hand, poring over a document that undoubtedly had been given the 'Maria treatment'. We gave each other a knowing look and I left. I was too angry to say anything.

Later that day, I was still fuming when Jack and I received an email from Maria. "Both, I am in an important meeting. Please send out to the client the amended version of the documents I left on your desk. I will be back by 9.30 p.m. See you then."

See you at 9.30 p.m.? For what? There was nothing that needed to be done on the transaction that day, and I certainly wasn't about to hang around. I decided to send the client my version of the document and then left at 7 p.m. having completed my tasks for that day.

I woke to discover an email sent at 1 a.m. from Maria to the partner in charge. The email read as follows,

"Dear Patrick,

Jack and I spent some time this evening putting together a potential agenda for the meeting next Friday with points to discuss. We will discuss with [me], whenever she gets in.

Kind regards,
Maria."

I had to smile. Maria was clearly trying to make me look bad. Why on earth the agenda for next week had to be discussed at 1 a.m. was beyond me. I was surprised, however, to learn that Jack had waited around on Maria's instructions.

The next day Maria came to my office. I expected her to scold me for ignoring her markup and for leaving early but she simply asked me to review something a trainee had drafted and then left.

Our next clash was to be more dramatic.

By the time I was 2 years qualified, I was used to interacting with clients on my own and had arranged to speak with our client concerning my workstream one afternoon. I was a little surprised when Maria turned up in my office ready for the call. She hadn't been invited but was obviously spying on my diary.

I had no objection; perhaps she wanted to be kept in the loop, I told myself. The client asked if he could start by asking a few questions. "Of course," I replied, and he proceeded to run through some points. I was about to open my mouth in response when Maria leant over and pressed the mute button on my office phone. "What are you going to say?" she asked. I was shocked. I pushed her finger away and responded to the client.

Another question… again, the finger on the mute button. I was furious and our client was puzzled by the long silences at my end. At this point, I simply got up and walked out. Maria called out, "Where are you going?" I replied, "Feel free to take over".

I bumped into Jack on my way back from the toilet. I often retreated there when I needed to calm down. Jack looked more red-faced and stressed out than ever. I mentioned what had happened and I was surprised to hear that Maria frequently interrupted his calls, either putting Jack on mute or undermining what he said. "This has got to stop. Enough is enough," I said.

"Don't be a martyr," Jack called after me.

I stomped into Maria's office ready for a confrontation. I was surprised when she raised her head and said, "I'm sorry, that was rude. Can we be friends again?" "Erm… sure. Don't worry about it," I said, taken aback.

I walked back to my desk, wondering if Maria had multiple personalities. If she did, I rather liked the one I had just met.

The transaction lasted just over a year. Maria and Jack worked late most nights and I left at a decent hour most of the time. I learned to ignore Maria's late-night non-urgent "urgent" emails. Maria learned to trust that I would get the job done. Jack, on the other hand, got to the point where he couldn't take anymore and left the firm shortly after we completed the deal.

I can't help but recall his words "don't be a martyr". I wish he had taken his own advice.

Moral of the story: People will get away with as much as you let them get away with. You have to set boundaries.

Chapter 7

All work and no lunch

In primary school, we are taught that human beings need certain basic things to flourish: we need water to keep hydrated, we need nourishment to grow and play games and we need human contact. It is amazing how our little brains grasp these concepts at such a young age and equally amazing how quickly we forget these basic concepts as adults.

During my time at the firm, I came across many colleagues who preferred to eat at their desks. Their reasons were many – some thought that an hour in the canteen was a waste of time, and, had they spent that hour working, they would get through the day faster. Surprisingly (or unsurprisingly), it was these individuals who ended up working late into the evening. I'm not sure whether the cause of this was inefficiency, fatigue, keenness or a combination. Speaking personally, I can say that on days when I did not move from my desk, time went by more slowly and I found it more difficult to concentrate.

The other advantage of having lunch in the canteen was, of course, human contact. I established close friendships at lunch. We discussed a mixture of law, politics, celebrity gossip and life. I often discovered that I was not alone in certain worries or struggles that I faced and lunchtime often became a therapy session. Colleagues might be working on similar transactions and lunchtime sessions also became a useful forum to discuss precedents and strategies.

I made it a point to send out a lunch email at 12.30 p.m. (I had a reminder in my calendar). This might sound silly, but the fact of the matter is that transactions sometimes take over your life. You live and breathe for that next email, the next phone call or comments on your draft document. Your diary can become so clogged up that it is too late by the time you realise you have not had time for lunch.

Your diet can become so dominated by "a quick fag to calm me down" or a "Diet Coke to pep me up" for the next meeting that by the time you realise it you have had five Diet Cokes and it is only 4 p.m.

I had only been qualified for 8 months when I realised, while on holiday and enjoying home-cooked food, just how erratic my meals had become. The Diet Cokes, cigarettes and copious amounts of coffee worked to suppress my appetite. I wasn't really exercising and, when I did eat, it was mainly junk food. I decided then that I had to start scheduling meals, drinks of water and gym sessions. When I came back to the firm, I got back in touch with my trainee lunch group and I never cancelled a session unless something dire happened (which it rarely ever does).

One spends so much time at the office that I decided that spending some time beautifying it and making it more 'homely' was a worthwhile investment. I bought a vase and some plastic flowers (I started out with the real ones but found that replacing them every week was a strain on time and resources).

I also realised that the air in the office is very dry. Most office buildings in London are air-conditioned and are devoid of any moisture whatsoever. My eyes felt dry and my skin looked nothing like it did in the smiling family picture that sat on my desk. So, I did a bit of research and found the solution - a humidifier. It was a funny-looking yellow round container with a little blow hole on the top. As soon as you turned it on, it released a stream of what the instructions described as "a cool mist". I got the first one past Health and Safety and then other friends followed suit. I must say that personally I thought it did wonders for my skin.

Moral of the story: Being a good lawyer doesn't entail self-deprivation. Lawyers are human beings too and we flourish when we are nourished, watered and when we live in a pleasant and nurturing environment. Sacrificing lunch may help you get a document out an hour early, and another Diet Coke may help you meet the target deadline of 4 p.m. However, in a world where demands are ever-increasing, no one will look out for you if you don't look out for yourself.

Chapter **8**

Great Expectations

Under-promise and overdeliver- words to live by.

Rex was a hard man to please and, as the name suggests, he was not a man you wanted to cross.

I hadn't really spoken with Rex outside social events and I doubted he even knew my name. Being a relatively senior partner in the team, he tended to work with the most senior associates. Anyway, I was happy to stay out of his way.

It was a Tuesday morning in mid-October. The junior associates were looking forward to the annual three-day refresher course conducted off-site. It was a rather dull course, covering all kinds of tedious topics. On the bright side, it meant three days out of the office.

My officemate and I were chatting away about the course conductor when the door sprang open and Rex bounded in. His beady eyes inspected us both. "I need you two on a new matter. Kick-off call is this afternoon at 2 p.m. Meet me in my office then." He then turned to leave, stopping to check our name plates outside the door. I wondered how he would decide which name belonged to which face.

Fifi sighed and said, "I hope it isn't too horrible - I hear he can be a real terror. Jody said he tends to speak in riddles and nothing you do is ever good enough".

Great, just when I thought it was going to be a good week.

2 p.m. came and Fifi and I settled in Rex's office, perched uncomfortably on two chairs that were set too high for our petite frames. I could feel my legs swinging uncomfortably below me – a throwback to the time my mother put me on the naughty stool. Notepads on our laps, we scribbled furiously as Rex discussed structuring ideas for the transaction.

The call lasted nearly three hours. Rex was clearly an extremely intelligent individual and Fifi and I scribbled away trying to keep up. The call ended rather abruptly and Rex then shooed us out of his office as he had another meeting to go to.

Exhausted, Fifi and I returned to our office and slumped into our chairs. "That was tough," Fifi said. I was about to respond when I heard a "ping" signalling the receipt of an email. The sound had come from both of our computers making me think it was one of those useless IT update emails. I turned to my screen to find an email from Rex addressed to both Fifi and myself.

It read; "I'm in another meeting. Fifi - please produce a short memo on the pros and cons of structuring the deal as a cross-border merger. [Me]- Please produce a short memo on using the alternative structuring option we discussed on the call. I'd like to see these by Friday morning".

Friday morning? Well, that wasn't going to be possible. We would be out of the office attending our training course for three days that week. And I had other urgent things to get on with in the meantime. Fifi looked up. "Hmm, I will do what I can today and see how it goes. I'll work around my other matters - he did say a *brief* memo."

Before I could respond, Fifi had "replied all" to Rex's email to say "Sure, I will fit this in around my other work and have it to you by Friday morning". I was a bit annoyed with her.

If I now said Friday wouldn't be possible, I risked being marked out as the lazy or incompetent roommate. Why did Fifi have to be such a suck-up?

I decided to mull over the task for a bit and see how it went before responding. A few hours later and I knew that the Friday deadline would be impossible to meet, unless, of course, I was willing to stay up all night. I had a choice - sleep or Rex? Comfortable bed or office desk? Should I show Rex how committed I was to the job or show him that I didn't care as much as Fifi?

A few minutes passed and I knew the answer.

I felt my cheeks flush as I really didn't want a confrontation with Rex. My fingers trembled a bit as I drafted and redrafted a hesitant response. My response was something along the lines of "Rex, I am due to attend a training course for the juniors over the next three days and will not have time to spend on the memo. I will get you a draft by the end of the day on Tuesday. Hope that's OK."

I felt a bit sick as I pressed send. I didn't have to wait long for a response. "Ping" and Rex's response had arrived. It simply read - "If that's the best you can do".

I didn't know what that meant - was there a deeper meaning? Was he annoyed? Had he agreed to my proposed deadline? I was too busy to ponder these questions for long. "Who cares if he is mad?" I thought. At least I had bought myself some time.

The next day, I woke up thankful that I would not be spending the day in the office being barked at by Rex. The course was uneventful but tiring and I was glad I hadn't volunteered to spend the evening drafting any memos. The next day was similarly uneventful.

On Friday afternoon, we were being talked at about accounting methods when I thought I spotted Fifi crying. I went to her during our break to see what the matter was. "I haven't managed to finish the memo for Rex," she said. "I was up all of last night working on it. Then this morning I got this." She passed me her phone. It was an angry email from Rex chasing Fifi for the memo that he had now promised to the client.

"Uh, nasty old man," I said. "He knows we are all attending this training course together. Just write back and explain that it is taking longer than expected."

I am not sure how Fifi dealt with Rex. Tuesday came and went and I emailed Rex my memo. There was no "thank you" or even acknowledgement of receipt, but then I really wasn't expecting it.

The weeks dragged on and there were more tasks from Rex. I soon became accustomed to his character – moody and unpredictable; he loved confrontation and challenged everything. On the flipside, he was brilliant and principled and his bark was worse than his bite. You always knew where you stood with him. If he was angry, believe you me, you would be the first to know.

Moral of the story: Law firms are places of great expectations. A skill that you will have to learn is managing those expectations. If you don't, you will find yourself in a world where slog as you may, nothing is ever good enough.

Part III

Old Hand

Chapter 9

I'm all yours

"Can you give an example of a time you demonstrated that you are a team player?" An annoying but frequently asked question on job application forms and at interviews.

But what does it really mean to be an effective team player?

It was a Tuesday. My first day back at the office after a three-week holiday. I expected it to be a pretty relaxed day and I hoped to get out early so I could unpack and sort out my flat.

As I went through my inbox, systematically highlighting all the useless newsletters for deletion, I felt a presence behind me. Then those dreaded words - "Do you have capacity?" Now, if you recall, I fall into a Type 3 personality and, as a rule, rarely say "yes". Well, having just returned from my holiday and ready to sink my teeth into something new, this time I said, "I'm all yours".

An hour later, I was invited to a meeting in Phil's office. Phil was the senior partner on the transaction and I would be working with another associate, Daisy. In a nutshell, our client was selling a multinational vaccines business to another company. The deadline for completion[4] was tight as our client was in a hurry to sell the business. Simple enough, right?

---

[4] The date the sale is officially done.

Several documents were involved in the sale including a sale and purchase agreement transferring the business assets (SPA), and a complex transitional services agreement.

For those of you unfamiliar, a transitional services agreement, or "TSA" for short, allows the buyer to receive certain services from the seller post-completion of the sale. In our case, we would be selling the vaccine manufacturing equipment and IP[5], but the buyer would need the support of the seller and their employees for a few months as they got the hang of the business.

The TSA detailed the equipment and service that our client would provide the buyer. The buyers naturally would want our client's employees to provide as much support as possible, for as long as possible and for as low a price as possible. Our task was to determine what support was vital and ensure that nothing in the drafting then allowed the buyers to take advantage of our client. The tricky part was that much of the drafting would need to capture specialist scientific and technological processes – not the forte of lawyers.

As a complete newcomer to the transaction, I was asked to read some background information. I was told that we would have the opportunity to discuss the TSA with our client in two days' time. I'd be assisting Daisy who had done a first draft of the TSA.

The next day, Phil called and asked, "Do you need a visa to go to France?"

---

[5] Intellectual Property.

"No," I replied. "Good; we leave on the 7 a.m. Eurostar to Paris. Bring an overnight bag." I hung up. The plan, I learned, was to have a face-to-face meeting with our client to discuss the draft documents. Phil would walk the General Counsel through the SPA, Daisy would lead the discussion on the TSA and I was to listen in for now so I could help her later on.

I was at St Pancras Station at 6.15 a.m. I had a small suitcase in which I had my pyjamas, an adaptor, laptop, numerous phones and chargers, underwear, a toothbrush, makeup and a change of clothes. I found my seat on the train.

Phil arrived next. Last boarding call and Daisy was nowhere to be seen. We tried her phone but there was no answer, then it was too late – we were off. Phil didn't look worried. "Never mind, she can catch the next train and be in Paris by the afternoon. We can start by talking through the SPA."

Twenty minutes later, an email from Daisy - "Phil, I'm very sorry I missed the train. I woke up with a massive headache and am not feeling well at all. I will try and make it to Paris by the afternoon". Then another email, this time from the client; "Morning, Phil. We hope to discuss the TSA and sale agreement concurrently this morning. I have another meeting at 12 and the engineers are tied up this afternoon too. Hope that's ok."

Phil sighed. Looking out at me above the rim of his spectacles, he said, "Looks like you have a lot to read through before we get to Paris". He handed me Daisy's TSA. Phil would be caught up in other meetings meaning I would have no backup.

However, I'd had very little background, I wasn't at all familiar with the manufacturing processes, and, in fact, I hardly knew anything about the business.

How do you react in a situation like that? I smiled, took the TSA he was holding out and began to read. I had a little under two hours and it was a 130-page document.

The devil is in the detail they say. This document was possessed. Every fifth sentence contained a word I had never heard of. It was like reading a different language. I looked out at the moving countryside. The sun was shining, some cows grazed lazily and I wondered what it might be like to live a quiet and peaceful life in one of the little farmhouses that flew past.

The train jerked me out of my daydream. I was never going to be able to absorb and understand all 130 pages by the time we arrived.

Do I tell Phil that this is ridiculous? Should I pretend that I too am unwell? I closed my eyes and I heard Phil's voice; "How are you getting on?" I opened my eyes. Phil looked worried as if he could read my mind. I smiled and said, "I'll do my best. Don't worry".

I cursed myself (and poor Daisy) as I shook hands with the engineers. What was I thinking? I was on my own now. No turning back. Each engineer had a copy of our draft document in front of him and they looked at me expectantly. I was half their age and so I already felt like I was on the back foot. I smiled and simply said, "I hope you agree with me that the document in front of you makes for some very dull reading. We lawyers can make anything sound boring but we do our best". One or two smiles, one or two unimpressed expressions and one or two engineers looked bored already.

I cleared my throat and ventured, "I know that the idea of today's meeting was to go through the draft in front of you, but it may be more helpful if we simply go through the headings and you explain the nature of the technology and some of the jargon to me. I would then ask that you allow me to ask some questions. I can deal with the boring legal drafting later to capture what you describe".

At this, the tension dissipated a bit and I saw more smiles and a hint of sympathy. One of the older engineers smiled and said, "That sounds like a plan. Some of the jargon still goes above my head".

I saw Phil later that evening at dinner. I had spent the afternoon putting into words the engineers' explanations and had a redraft of the TSA up and running. Phil was a man of few words but his smile that evening said everything.

Daisy stayed back in London and I took the TSA over from her. Phil thought it would be easier that way since I had "made friends" with the engineers. The transaction was far from painless and we spent many long nights negotiating with the other side. During the negotiations, I had the advantage of understanding the technology in question far better than the other side's lawyers (having had a crash course on the technology) and had become real friends with the team of engineers.

The story does have a happy ending. The transaction closed according to plan and I was treated to one of the most extravagant lunches I have ever had in Paris. In fact, I got the day off just to travel to Paris and back for lunch.

Moral of the story: Teamwork is not just about doing your bit. It is about being willing to put yourself out there and do other peoples' bits too. I have come to realise that especially with more complex transactions, ones that are trailblazers, even the partners in all their wisdom don't have all the answers.

CHAPTER **10**

How to sleep with the lights on

I have had my fair share of all-nighters. Like doctors, lawyers can sometimes be on-call during the night, not for a medical emergency but for a 'document emergency'.

Picture this; you have been assigned to a deal - Rose plc is acquiring Lily plc (I do love flowers). You are acting for Rose plc (a slightly prettier flower in my view). You attend the kick-off call and discuss how the purchase will be structured. You also discuss the all-important timetable. This timetable will determine your life for the next few months so you listen carefully.

4:00 p.m. Friday 23rd May. The day and time are burned into your memory. This is the day it will all be over and you can have a nice celebration; maybe even have a few days off.

The months drag on. There are good days and bad. On good days, you are left to get on with your work during the day, and, if you are lucky, you get out of the office at a reasonable hour.

Any number of things can happen on a bad day: (i) you are constantly pestered by Lily's lawyers - you will have to stay late due to all their constant distractions during the day; or (ii) you find out that, unbeknownst to you, the bankers on the transaction have been working out a side deal – more bedtime reading, more documents to produce; or (iii) the deal structure changes. Again, more bedtime reading and more documents for you to produce.

Then suddenly, two words: "pens down".

I was in my second seat when I first heard those words and I thought they were glorious. I was told that Rose plc had reached an impasse with the other side and the deal had collapsed. It was like a fairy godmother had appeared to me and waved her magic wand making all my troubles go away. I could go to the ball after all and did not have to play Cinderella reviewing documents all night.

I decided to take a walk to get some fresh air and texted my friend saying that I would be out early that day and we should go out for dinner. I booked a table at our favourite restaurant and left the office at 6 p.m. I met my friend at the tube station and we went for cocktails first, followed by dinner. It was 10.30 p.m. when my phone rang. The deal was back on and with a vengeance. In return for some concessions from Lily, our client had graciously promised that his lawyers would have all the documents reviewed by 9 a.m. the next morning.

Back to the office I trudged, hoping the effects of the cocktails would wear off quickly.

As you will recall, the long-anticipated signing of the Rose deal was scheduled for 4 p.m. on Friday 23rd May. Friday 23rd May – a date set in stone from the beginning of the transaction, a date that I had written into various documents and had been repeated like a mantra on countless phone calls.

23rd May, the day I'd be set free. By the way, why 4 p.m.? The CEO of Rose plc had to attend his daughter's school play.

The lawyers and bankers had been beavering away and the countdown finally began.

Note to the reader: this may make for boring reading but it gives you an idea of what usually happens to deal timetables at the last minute.

Thursday, 22nd May 9:00 a.m. An "all parties call"[6] is scheduled to discuss any outstanding points and to try and get them agreed.

I am in the senior partner's room. He dials into the conference call and mutes the phone while we all chat away happily waiting for the other parties to join. A few others join but then an email appears in our inboxes saying Mr Smith (lead lawyer for Lily) has been delayed and can we do the call a bit later in the day. Annoying but not disastrous as there is not much left to discuss.

Thursday, 22nd May 4.30 p.m. All parties call rescheduled for this time. Again, we all gather in the senior partner's room waiting to get the deal over with so we could celebrate. As we wait, again an email from Mr Smith. The email, to everyone's confoundment, lists out various new demands. The email says that Lily may pull out of the deal if these are not met.

---

[6] A conference call with all parties involved attending (lawyers, bankers, clients, etc)

What to do? Jake, a partner with many years of experience, is clearly annoyed but not wholly surprised.

We call our client at Rose. He is furious about all the demands that Mr Smith and Lily are making. Rose asks Jake for his opinion.

Jake thinks that the demands will have tax implications. We will need to discuss this with the tax partner. We will also need to discuss it with our Dubai office as some of the demands relate to overseas assets.

Thursday 22nd May 5 p.m. Our colleagues in Dubai have gone home for the day. We leave a voice message scheduling a call for early the next morning, apologising for infringing on their weekend which has already begun. We try our tax partner and he says he will need time to consider.

Friday 23rd May 6.30 a.m. Our Dubai colleagues have come up with a strategy and wish to discuss this with Lily.

Friday 23rd May 11 a.m. Lily won't budge and refuse to hear out our Dubai colleagues. Not only that, they now have more demands.

4 p.m. on Friday 23 May comes and goes.

Friday 23rd May 8 p.m. Rose and Lily have managed to agree some of the points relating to the overseas assets. Lily say they will send us 'a document', 'shortly'. I will have to do a first review when it arrives.

Friday 23rd May Dinner time comes and goes. I had decided to avoid canteen food at dinner time - the food is never great, especially on a Friday evening. Specialities included meatball curry (sometimes the spaghetti that had gone with said recycled meatballs at lunch found their way into the curry too) and rice salad (made from the previous day's leftover biryani).

I had hoped that the document would arrive in time to allow me to go home for dinner. By 10 p.m., when my poor stomach tires of grumbling, it is too late. The canteen is now closed.

Friday 23rd May 10.45 p.m. Annoyed that it is taking so long, I call the other side. I am assured the document will arrive 'soon'.

Saturday 24th May 1 a.m. I finally hear a "ding" indicating the arrival of a new email. I look up at my computer screen. Finally, an end to this evening of torture!

False alarm - it is an update from the IT department letting me know that all computers will shut down automatically at 4 a.m. and that anyone still working should save their work. Frustrated, I delete the email and walk over to the meeting room.

I have my Blackberry on full volume in case an email should finally arrive, and I lie down on the couch. Tired and hungry, I decide that I had better get an hour's sleep as it is now likely to be a long night.

I close my eyes but the surgical-grade lights in the room are too bright to allow me to doze off. I get up again. Where is the light switch? There isn't one. The lights are motion-sensitive. I lie back down again, annoyed, and try to be as still as possible. 15 minutes and 900 sheep later the lights go off – finally.

I close my eyes again and just as I am about to doze off there is a noise in the corridor. The overnight cleaners are vacuuming. Another few minutes go by and I hear the door to the meeting room open. The lights jump back to life triumphantly as a cleaner peers in, apologises, and leaves.

Saturday 24th May 4.30 a.m. The document finally arrive. I have to restart my computer, of course, as forewarned by the IT department.

Reading it, my heart sinks as it contains a number of changes, which I know we would not be able to accept. A ping-pong battle ensues. The document goes back and forth between us and Lily's lawyers for the next two days.

The agreement is only signed on Monday 26th May at 10 a.m.

They say that necessity is the mother of invention and that long weekend taught me a great life skill. I had discovered that my hair could double up as an eye mask. The lights no longer bothered me and neither did the cleaners.

Moral of the story: Long hair can be a great asset. It can be used as a scarf or shawl when the aircon is turned up too high. It can be used to swat insects, as camouflage or fancy dress if draped over the face and it can of course also be used as eye masks when you find yourself unable to sleep in an airport or indeed a law firm.

More serious moral: It ain't over till it's over. Be prepared for anything.

Chapter 11

Rules of engagement

Working at a law firm is like being in a relationship. There are a few rules to abide by to ensure the relationship does not collapse:

Rule 1: The wrong way to manage the relationship is to ask yourself each morning whether you should be in it in the first place.

I have to say that I never woke up and thought to myself "I can't wait to jump out of bed and trot off to work". On the other hand, I never woke up thinking "I hope I get hit by a bus so I have an excuse not to go to work"- something a friend of mine admitted to doing. Most mornings I simply got on with it. I made a mental list of all the things I needed to do that morning, dressed and set off to work.

Focussing on the task at hand, I found, can serve to distract you from all the negative thoughts that can otherwise fill the mind. Now, I have to say that I had a lucky strike with my supervisors as a trainee and with the partners I worked for as an associate. None were malevolent as such and none made me dread coming into work.

What happens when you have the misfortune of working with a truly nasty character?

As a trainee, this can be tricky, as you have little choice as to the supervisor you sit with. In such a situation, I would recommend the 'grin and bear it' approach.

Complaining or confronting is unlikely to change things. Don't forget that it is likely that the nasty character has had many trainees before you and if no one else managed to change them, and if complaints from previous trainees fell on deaf ears, it is unlikely that a complaint or confrontation from you will make a difference.

Do your best and remember that you only need to spend a few months with the person. Remember to also try and work with other people in the department as you do not want your experience to be tainted by one bad apple.

I have often advised trainees not to choose a department for qualification based on people. People are transient - good-natured persons can leave and easily be replaced by those who are not so good-natured.

And, if you find yourself working with a nasty character as an associate?

As an associate, you need to learn to stand your ground. You may come across as impertinent sometimes but better to be impertinent than weak – people will learn to respect you for it.

Now, I'm not suggesting you go looking for a fight. What I am saying is that if you think you are right, don't let anyone convince you that you are wrong. Of course, do your research and when proven wrong, gracefully accept that you were mistaken, but never show fear and be prepared to argue your point of view. Remember - in most cases, there is no single right answer.

Rule 2: Don't wash your dirty laundry in public.

In my relationship with my now fiancé, I have always believed that any problems, disagreements or misunderstandings are best dealt with by a direct face-to-face discussion and should be dealt with as quickly as possible. I have friends who like to engage in protracted discussions regarding their other halves. These friends shop for opinions on what the other person "meant when he said" or "how should I broach the subject" or "can you believe he did that to me? What should I do now?"

As a rule, when writing official mid-year and end-of-year reviews for trainees, I have never had anything negative to say. Now, you might argue that this is far from constructive. No one is perfect and we only learn when our flaws are pointed out and we have the opportunity to ponder them and try and do better next time. I completely agree.

My approach was to point out flaws face-to-face. If someone did something that annoyed me or did not do something to the standard I expected, I pointed it out there and then. It made for uncomfortable conversation sometimes but it meant that by the time a review came about, the person in question had had time to try and improve themselves. As a trainee, the people I found most difficult to work with were the associates who chatted a lot, told me I was doing well and then wrote stingy or negative reviews.

A consequence of this was that I was very popular with the trainees in my department. I was not trying to win any popularity awards, it was simply my way, but I always had someone happy to help out when I needed a hand. They knew they could count on me to be fair and that they would learn from the experience.

Rule 3: Knock and the door will be opened

Mary was extremely hardworking, diligent and focused. We became quite close and I would sometimes pop by her office in the afternoon to say hello. Each time I popped by, Mary seemed to be suffering from some form of illness. She looked tired, red-eyed and generally had some complaint or the other. "I was here all of last weekend again," she would say; or "I am the only associate on this deal and it's just too much for one person to handle"; or "I worked all of last month. Not one weekend off and I haven't been offered a single day off in lieu".

Mopey Mary lived alone with her cat. I had seen pictures and even the cat looked pathetic – no doubt deprived of company and care while Mary slaved away in the office.

At first, I felt sorry for Mary, thinking that she was extremely unlucky. Either that or she was a victim of her own competence. But then it so happened that Mary and I came to work as juniors on the same deal.

Each of us was responsible for coordinating a separate due diligence workstream. That is to say, we had roughly the same type and quantity of work and had to work to roughly the same deadlines.

My Step 1: Calculating that we had about 200 documents to review in about a week (this was just the first batch of course), I asked the lead partner to allocate me two trainees to assist full-time. I met with the trainees at midday and we started work that afternoon.

By the end of the week, we had reviewed the first batch of documents and looked forward to a weekend of peace.

Mary's step 1: After an hour of procrastination and complaining to her roommate about how unfair it was that she was on the deal, she began reviewing the documents herself. Realising that she probably needed assistance, she decided to send out an email asking the trainees if anyone was free for a few hours to assist her.

Sending out such an email late in the afternoon, by the way, is not a great idea - most people are usually already occupied on something by then or have had enough of the office for a day and want to go home early.

She had one response and scheduled a meeting with the trainee for later that afternoon. Mary had a habit of underestimating the time something would take and didn't take much notice when the trainee said that the task would definitely require him to spend more than just a few hours on it as Mary had suggested in her original email. Again, big mistake; always overestimate rather than underestimate the time something will take - no one will thank you for ruining their evening. Anyway, Mary and the trainee worked the weekend and finished reviewing their batch in time for Monday - in time to be presented with the next batch.

By Monday, the trainees I had been assigned were comfortable with what needed to be done and they were finished with the second batch of documents by Thursday. Mary, on the other hand, her reputation deteriorating amongst the trainees, laboured on, on her own, complaining as she went.

By the end of the deal, Mary and I had managed to get through about 5 batches of documents. I had worked one weekend and she had worked 4 weekends. I had organised a 'picnic' in the office to keep our morale up on the one weekend we worked. Mopey Mary complained but said she dare not order in as the food was too expensive and the partner in charge might get annoyed (because that was how she thought partners were).

With all documents finally reviewed, I spoke with the partner in charge and requested a day in lieu for myself and the two trainees. "No problem. I'll arrange it," was all he said. That was that.

Finding that she was not offered a day in lieu (as she hadn't asked), Mary sulked and complained but of course, nothing really changed.

Moral of the story:

1) Be nice to people and they will be nice to you. Having a reputation for being good at your job will take you far. Having a reputation for being good at your job and being a nice person will take you further.

2) Don't send emails asking trainees for help just as people are winding down and getting ready to go home. Plan your work early and be reasonable.

3) Better to overestimate the amount of resource you need than to underestimate it.

4) Ask for help. No one is going to steal your glory. If you don't ask for help, you are in danger of robbing yourself of precious downtime.

Chapter 12

Pro-bono

"I want to be a lawyer because I believe that a strong legal system is the foundation of society. I want to be part of the machine that ensures that justice is available to all in equal measure."

It seems a very long time ago now that I was writing my personal statement at high school. My careers councillor said the opening paragraph (typed above) was too idealistic. It was the first thing she deleted.

I never mentioned my ideological ideas again either in application forms or in interviews, but that did not mean that such ideas were dead. I did, and do, want to make a difference - who doesn't? So, when the opportunity arose, I signed up to work evenings pro bono at the local Law Centre.

My first evening at the Law Centre. I expected to walk into a building that would be buzzing with activity, to meet the real hard-core lawyers and see them in action fighting for people's civil rights. Instead, I was led to a small run-down building located right next to a dubious-looking chicken shop on the outskirts of the borough. We pressed the buzzer several times before the door was finally opened by a heavily pregnant woman.

Maura was a plump, smiley woman. "Sorry," she said as she opened the door. "I'm a bit of a one-woman band around here. Please come in."

I was led through a waiting room occupied by two ladies, who, I was told, were the clients. "Only two people have turned up so far," Maura said, "but we are expecting at least another three".

Miriam and Ed, who had worked with the waiting clients previously, picked up their files and led the two ladies into a meeting room. Maura handed me another file and said, "This belongs to Mr Hari. He should be here any minute. Will you have a read through it in the meantime?"

I took the file to a corner of the room and opened it. It was falling to pieces and contained about 20 scraps of paper, most of which I could not make head or tail of as the notes were all handwritten and the writing was terrible. I had managed to get the gist of the claim when Mr Hari arrived.

Mr Hari seemed a bit disappointed to see me. "Every time I come here I see someone new." I felt for him. I'd be annoyed too. I apologised and said, "Do you mind going over your claim with me?" He sighed. "Sure. This must be the tenth time I am having to recount my story". Mr Hari was an elderly man; in fact, a very elderly man. It appeared that he had made a late payment on his telephone bill and the company had disconnected the telephone. Although payment had since been made, his landline still wasn't working.

This seemed a simple enough case. I tried the telephone company from the Law Centre and, as usual, was put on hold for half an hour. The company insisted the phone was now working. After a long argument, they promised to have someone check it the next day.

Poor Mr Hari. He explained that this had happened several times. The company had promised to check his phone, then a maintenance person would arrive and say that they needed some tools and would make another appointment to come back but, without a working phone, no one could reach Mr Hari to make the new appointment.

In addition, without a working phone at home, the almost 80-year-old Mr Hari was having to walk to the nearest payphone in all manner of weather to try and make an appointment with the Law Centre.

Angered, I took down his address and promised I would do my best to sort things out. When Mr Hari left, I spoke with Maura. "Can you send one of your team over to check on him tomorrow?" I asked, "just to make sure that the phone company has actually done their job?" She smiled, hand on her round belly, and said, "We just don't have the budget for house calls".

Frustrated, I left wondering what I could do. The next evening, I called the phone company but they refused to speak with me without Mr Hari present. I went back to the Law Centre the next week and decided to visit Mr Hari as he lived only a few blocks away. I took another colleague with me as I did not want to walk past the chicken shop alone after dark - call me crazy.

Mr Hari was a bit surprised to see us and told us that his phone was still not working. Same thing - an engineer had come, said he needed some special tool and said he would come back but didn't. I called the phone company and they confirmed the story saying that the engineer was unable to book an appointment.

"Of course he wasn't!" I shouted. "Don't you people make any notes? This man is old. He doesn't have a working phone and doesn't have access to email. If this goes on, I will file a formal complaint." We were promised that an engineer would visit the next morning and would make a record of the equipment he needed so that the next engineer would come prepared. I took down the name of the person I was speaking with, threatening a personal complaint if the correct instructions were not passed on to the engineer.

A week later and Mr Hari's phone was finally fixed. I hadn't used any legal skills. I hadn't worked on a cutting-edge, trail-blazing transaction. However, the satisfaction I got from seeing that poor old man with a working phone was far greater than the satisfaction I got from any other deal I have worked on.

Moral of the Story: As lawyers, we are perfectionists living in a world of imperfection. We expect everyone and everything around us to operate with the same standard of diligence and attention to detail that we impose on ourselves.

The moral of the story here is that sometimes you just have to cope with imperfection and do your best. This applies especially to pro bono opportunities. Law Centres are not law firms. They are run with tiny budgets and people simply have to do the best they can. This does not however mean that they are not worthy causes and sometimes the greatest skill you can learn is to do the best you can with few resources.

Pro-bono

I helped out on various other pro bono projects during my time at the firm. I met several people I would never have otherwise come across, I developed skill sets I would not have developed at the firm, and although I was often frustrated because things rarely went right, when they did, it was an amazing feeling.

Part IV

The Flipside

CHAPTER **13**

Embrace the unknown

The unknown can make us uncomfortable. I've learned over the years that you have to embrace uncomfortable situations, for these are the experiences you learn the most from.

The transaction I had been working on had just completed and I was having a quiet week in the office. This is the most vulnerable time for any associate. The deal that had so far protected me from being given further work was no more. I was a sitting duck.

I sat, browsing the web – a rather dangerous activity. A partner catching someone in the act will immediately bound back to his desk and send out an email to his comrades in the group demanding that they immediately supply the offender with more work. "We don't pay these people to surf the net!"

My screen was partly shielded by the doorframe, but could still be seen clearly from one side through a wall of glass. I had partially solved that problem by sticking up some strategically placed structure charts on the glass. The only problem was that I am not very tall and, although the charts were cleverly placed in a view-obstructing column, a person tall enough could just about see over the column.

That is all to say that I was browsing somewhat cautiously, finger at all times on the mouse and ready to click on a boring-looking pdf that I kept minimised and ready for when I heard footsteps behind me.

Hearing a click, click of shoes, I immediately clicked into the pdf and pretended to be absorbed. Then someone entered my office. I looked around, breath held, hoping that the next deal I was put on wasn't something horrible, but it was only Roy. Roy was the person in charge of delivering letters and parcels to our offices and he was holding a large box.

I took the box, signed for it and tore it open. In it was my first "tombstone" – or what normal people would, in a more positive manner, call a memento. It was a beautiful cut-glass object with my name and the name and a description of the deal on it.

I was so proud. I was the first associate at my level in the group to get a tombstone and I placed it on a high shelf so it could clearly be seen by any passers-by (above my obstructing column of structure charts) in the corridor.

As I sat staring at my tombstone, I heard another set of footsteps approaching. I spun around, again feeling a knot in my stomach. I saw the tall figure of Mike approaching.

Mike was a youngish, straight-talking partner. I had worked with Mike before and he wasn't so bad.

Mike walked into my office and shut the door. He took off his glasses and began giving them a good scrub.

I hated the suspense. When he was finally satisfied with his spectacles, he put them back on, looked up and smiled. "I have an offer for you," he said. "What on earth is he on about?" I wondered. "An offer?" I queried.

"Yes. I have a client who is looking for someone to help them with a transaction. The catch is that you will be seconded to them as they want help from the inside."

"Who is the client? And what's the transaction?" I asked. Mike had a number of private equity clients and I didn't relish the idea of slogging away in some outpost on a transaction involving a new kind of intangible asset that I did not understand.

"It's a confectionery business called SweetNes," he responded. "Not one of our major clients but we have had a long-standing relationship with them and I know the General Counsel very well. They are doing an IPO[7]. The internal legal team is tiny and they want to bring in someone to assist with the prospectus."

"What's the catch?" I asked. Mike gave me a knowing smile. "Well, the team is very small, so there will be plenty to do. Also, the client is based in Slough." His voice trailed off so I didn't quite catch the last word.

"Sorry, where?" "Erm, Slough, but we will reimburse all your travel expenses and the working hours will be great," he said quickly.

I must admit that I was sceptical and Mike must have registered this. "Sleep on it," he said. At the time, I had not really considered the option of a secondment and did not

---

[7] Initial public offering. This is when a private company offers shares to the public in a new stock issuance. It's a pretty big deal for the company and it needs to publish a prospectus describing the business, assets, liabilities, risks, etc.

know what to expect. Having qualified relatively recently, the last thing I wanted to do was to get sent somewhere for six months, only to come back and discover that I had missed out on the real action and forgotten everything I had learned in the meantime.

I spent some time thinking about it and, after some negotiations with Mike, it was settled that I would go on a trial period. If I didn't like it, I could come back.

I am ashamed to say that in all my years living in London, I had rarely ventured past Zone 2. On my first day at SweetNes, I managed to catch the long train that took an hour and a half instead of the alternative hour-long journey.

I arrived in a huff and asked for Jake, the General Counsel. I took a seat and looked around. The SweetNes reception was adorned with all manner of model cakes and sweet jars. I was surrounded by colourful boiled sweets, candy canes and stripy peppermints.

Great - my fellow associates would no doubt be working on some hard-core cross-border deal of the year, while I was here playing Hansel and Gretel for six months.

Just as I was beginning to forget my train journey over and letting my imagination run away with me, Jake walked in. Jake was middle-aged and had a pleasant, trusting face. We introduced ourselves and he took me upstairs. I was pleasantly surprised to find that I had my own office. You will find that most office buildings in the City are open plan, with only the most senior individuals having their own offices. Law firms have traditionally been the exception to this rule and most still provide individual offices for their employees, but even this is now changing.

I was told that I had been given my own office due to the sensitive nature of Project Gingerbread and that my office would be used as the hub for anything related to it.

I walked into my office feeling a little important. This sensation soon disappeared as I turned on the lights and was mortified as the green glare hit me. I was to occupy a room called the "Peppermint Forest". Each office and meeting room in the building, I was told, was similarly themed. Everything in the room was vomit green and I was to sit on a "toadstool" in the middle of what looked like a candy forest. I am not going to last long, I thought as I sat down on my toadstool. How on earth could I take all this seriously?

I spent the first half of the day working out the IT system which was a lot less sophisticated than the system at the firm. There were none of the legal research portals I had become accustomed to while at the firm and I started to feel doom and gloom descending.

It was about 3 p.m. that afternoon when Jake walked in. He was smiling and said, "How do you like your office?" "It's interesting," I replied, faking a smile. He laughed and then proceeded to brief me on the transaction. I was told that only the most senior people in the business knew about it as it was still only at the infant stage. I should therefore refrain from discussing it more generally.

I was then taken around the floor and introduced to the executive team - all the top guys, essentially. I must admit that from the couple of hours I spent speaking with the executive team, I gained an amazing amount of insight into how the business operated. Each person was keen to talk about his role and the part of the business he/she was in charge of.

By the end of the day, I knew more about SweetNes than I did about any other client I had worked for previously.

Drafting the prospectus required me to describe the business, the assets, liabilities and risks to the business. I spent hours with the CEO, the CFO, the director for international business, the GC and the HR director. I got given tours of the factory and sampled the products. I witnessed the manufacturing process and both read and tasted the IP.

Looking back, I could have done the safe thing and stayed in my fancy office. But I would never have been given the kind of insight I gained during my time at Peppermint Forest headquarters.

Moral of the story: Embrace the unknown and the uncomfortable. Make use of every opportunity that is given to you, for each new opportunity will teach you something new if you are willing to learn.

Chapter 14

Make sure the shoe fits

I learned many things during my time working on Project Gingerbread. One lesson stood out and has held me in very good stead ever since - the true meaning of commercial awareness.

Commercial awareness took on a whole new meaning during my secondment. It is drilled into every budding trainee's head that a good lawyer needs to be 'commercially aware'. We are told that we should "read the FT", "watch the news" and "keep up to date with what is happening in the markets".

I always found all this mostly rather dull and can safely say that I never considered myself particularly commercially aware. However, I soon learned the true meaning of commercial awareness.

One of my tasks was to work through a "due diligence questionnaire". It was a relatively standard questionnaire that law firms often send their clients to get the materials they need for the prospectus. I now found myself on the other side of the questionnaire. It read something like this:

"Please provide:

1) all property deeds;
2) all relevant commercial contracts;

3) all intellectual property agreements;
4) all bank loans..."

My first step was to discuss the list with the legal team at SweetNes.

We each perched on a toadstool in Peppermint Forest and ran through the list. "The property deeds is an easy one," Jake said. "There's just the one factory in the UK and we have 5 buildings overseas. The bank loans are also fine as there aren't many."

"But, what do you mean by all relevant contracts? We have hundreds of agreements ranging from large supply agreements to agreements with our cleaners. Similarly, there is a vast amount of IP." Here is where the challenge arose.

While a statement such as "all commercial contracts entered into with the business" seems simple and clear enough, when you put it into context, it means very little. To demonstrate the difficulty SweetNes would have in complying with such a request, I was taken down to the "Dungeon"- a windowless, forgotten room in the basement where hundreds and hundreds of documents were filed away in fire-proof cabinets. "Unless you are suggesting we have some kind of massive document dump, I think we have a problem," said Jake.

Back at Peppermint Forest headquarters, Jake and I discussed ways of narrowing down the list of documents to something more practical. Clearly, a materiality threshold would need to be applied so that we could filter out the important contracts from the rest.

But even that did not really simplify things. What materiality threshold should be applied? "Material" strategically or financially? Do we mean material in a particular country or at a particular time? How far back or indeed forward in time do we go?

The task was mammoth. I had to speak with every commercial team in the company to get an idea of what they saw as being their most important contracts. A further complication was keeping the project a secret.

Sitting on my toadstool in the heart of my Peppermint Forest, I constantly demanded information from people in the business but could not say why I needed it or why it was so urgent. Safe to assume I did not win any popularity contests.

What I thought would be a simple task of collecting maybe 50 agreements turned into a leviathan. I couldn't help but feel that if the original questionnaire had been drafted more carefully, a lot of pain could have been avoided.

There were many instances during my secondment when I came to appreciate that commercial awareness doesn't mean reading the FT or understanding the markets, or, if it does, then that is only a small part of it. Commercial awareness means putting legal advice and instructions into the context of a business. It is easy to give broad or general advice and instructions or ask vague questions, but if they make no sense in the specific context or are too difficult to comply with, then they are of very little use.

Commercial awareness means making sure the shoe fits.

Moral of the story:

1) Upon returning from my secondment, I felt like I understood my clients and their needs like I never did before.
2) Sure, I hadn't worked on the sexiest transaction, but I felt like my experience had taught me something I could never have learned at the firm - how to think like the client. As a consequence, my advice on future transactions became more commercial. I knew what questions to ask and, most importantly, I was able to put myself in my clients' shoes, something they really appreciated.

CHAPTER **15**

No frills

As a lawyer in a big firm, you can sometimes feel like the high-flying heart specialist who has scores of medical degrees but who can't treat the common cold.

While I had plenty of experience working on large-scale, complex transactions, I had come to realise that I had little feel for the more day-to-day legal issues faced by SweetNes.

The days had flown by and Project Gingerbread was a success. I had become the queen of my Peppermint Forest. Jake and I had worked well together. I decided to suggest that I stay on at SweetNes for a little while longer to assist the legal team. I explained that I wanted to get a feel for real in-house work. Jake was only too happy to oblige and we arranged a short extension with Mike.

Super-secret project over, I was looking forward to getting down and dirty in the real world of an in-house lawyer. I was soon to discover that, as with everything in life, the in-house life was full of ups and downs.

First "down" - I lost my "Peppermint Forest". I was moved into an open plan station amongst the rest of the staff. I soon found that in this setting, the IT Helpline was much less inclined to treat any of my IT issues with the urgency they deserved. I was just another employee now and not the mysterious, youthful-looking consultant everyone had been talking about.

In addition, I was now working in very unfamiliar territory with few facilities to lean upon. I was asked all manner of questions and had all kinds of weird and wonderful ideas run past me for "sign-off".

Amusing example number 1: Sitting at my desk one morning, the phone rang. I picked up and an excited voice was on the other line. "Hi, I'm Laura from marketing. I have a great idea I just need you to quickly sign off on. Are you the correct person to speak to?"

"Well, I'm part of the legal team, so I may be able to help. What's the idea?" I asked.

"I just spoke with a clothing company called "BeFree". They want to place leaflets in our delivery packages and will pay us £10,000 a month to do so. It will be a great revenue stream! I just need you to sign off. I'll send the paperwork over now."

"Hold on a sec," I said. "I'll need a bit more information before I can sign off on this. Can you come over to the meeting room and have a chat? If I could see a sample of the leaflet that would be great too."

The meeting was highly entertaining. BeFree, it turned out, was a saucy lingerie company. The leaflet, which Laura had the company email her just before the meeting, contained pictures that we both agreed would be inappropriate additions to our delivery packages, many of which contained birthday hampers destined for children's birthday parties. Laura had only just been hired and wanted to make an impression. We agreed that she would drop the idea of the leaflets and would do more thorough research in the future. I agreed not to mention the embarrassing affair again.

Amusing example number 2: It was my first week in my new position as part of the in-house team and I had been firefighting emails all morning. I was always busy during the day, but this day had been particularly busy. As I sat, bashing out an email advising on the termination provision[8] someone had asked me to look at, I suddenly got an email.

The email was marked High Importance. Email subject: Very Urgent. Email message: I need to discuss something super urgent ASAP. A calendar invite promptly popped into my diary for that afternoon.

What on earth could this be about? Was it some disaster? Who was the person sending me the email and why was I the only one on the email if it was a disaster?

I could access an internal telephone directory on the computer, so I looked up the sender. Her name was Rhonda and she was from the IT team.

"Oh no!" I thought. "I hope this isn't an IT disaster." I was not an IT expert, but I knew full well that the smallest of issues with the IT system could have disastrous consequences for any organisation. I thought I might faint with all the anticipation so I decided to give Rhonda a call to ask her what this was all about.

I rang the extension and a panicky, hurried voice came on the line. "Hi, Rhonda?" I said. "You sent me an email saying

---

[8] A contractual clause setting out how a contract can be terminated.

you had something very urgent to discuss this afternoon. May I ask what it's about? You see, I have several other meetings scheduled, which I would need to cancel if you really think that is necessary."

"I can't really speak now," Rhonda's voice crackled. "I tried Lizzie's number earlier and she said she wasn't around this afternoon and neither is the GC so I would need to speak with you. I'll come round this afternoon." She hung up.

Lizzie was the other lawyer on the team. It was true that Lizzie and Jake were away that afternoon delivering a presentation to the Board of Directors. Great; so, the one day no one else is around, a disaster comes up.

The clock ticked time away and I found myself unable to concentrate on anything. I wanted to know what the disaster was. I wanted to know if I should start reading up on IT law or on the company's IT policy. I did both.

I had cancelled all my other supposedly "urgent" afternoon meetings as I knew what they were about and I knew that they weren't really all that urgent.

As the sun sank lower in the sky, so the knot moved lower in my stomach. Where was Rhonda? Perhaps the disaster was worse than I expected. Perhaps SweetNes was under cyber-attack and hundreds of bytes of sensitive information were being siphoned off to some remote, dark warehouse set up by a competitor.

I was about to call Rhonda to ask her where she was when she finally walked into my room. She looked tired and harried - not a good sign at all.

No frills

"Is everything ok?" I squeaked. I was so afraid that the words hardly came out. "Yes. I'm just so tired and there is so much to do."

I could hardly contain myself. "Go on," I said nervously.

"Well, we have this IT software supplier. They provided us with a piece of software that allows us to match products with particular factories. It is a pretty important piece of software. The licence is due to expire and we had forgotten all about it. We need to put together a renewal agreement and it needs to be agreed by tomorrow morning at the latest."

I was relieved. This was not the disaster I had thought it was. Nevertheless, renewal agreements usually take a while to negotiate and, if Rhonda was saying she needed it to be put in place in a day, I didn't have much time at all.

"Can you send me the existing licence agreement?" I asked. "Sure." I waited another two hours before the licence agreement arrived. I was a bit annoyed and printed it off immediately. The first thing I looked at was the expiry date. It was in three weeks! So why were we working to a deadline of the next morning?

I was about to call Rhonda again when Lizzie walked in. "Sorry, I've been so tied up today. It's been a long day with the Board Meeting. Everything ok?"

"Yes," I said and I explained Rhonda's emails and the licence agreement.

Lizzie laughed. "Sorry," she said. "I meant to send you an email to warn you. Rhonda is going on holiday for three weeks and I thought she might pull something like this. She just wants to be able to say to her boss that it has all been sorted before she leaves. It's not urgent, don't worry. Her boss will just have to cover for her and help us negotiate the agreement."

I felt so silly, and so used! Did Rhonda think that I had nothing better to do? I had cancelled all my meetings and procrastinated so much that I hadn't got anything else done that afternoon. I would be more wary the next time someone said something is "urgent".

Moral of the story:

1) At a law firm, lawyers are the breadwinners. Consequently, everything in a law firm is centred around the lawyers and their needs and comfort. In a business, the commercial guys bring in the money and they run the show. The lawyers are simply a hurdle that people need to get over, and you get treated accordingly. So be prepared for that.

2) At a law firm, you meet resistance from the opposing team. The enemy is outside your walls. In-house, the enemy is sometimes within your walls. I found that a lack of understanding or a lack of caring (or both) for legal issues in-house can sometimes make it very difficult to negotiate points that don't have an obvious commercial bearing. The commercial teams simply want to get a project done so that fiscal targets can be met and this can sometimes prove to be very frustrating as it dilutes your bargaining position as a lawyer.

3) At a law firm, you generally work with other lawyers who understand and are familiar with legal concepts. In-house you come across a variety of individuals, some with more of a feel for the law than others. I found that I had to adjust my communication style accordingly and sometimes innovate; again, not always easy to do, especially if you are dealing with people with short attention spans.

Chapter 16

The grass looks greener

The world of law firms is shrouded in mystery.

Rumours abound amongst the eager university graduates who are ready to embark on their legal journeys. Here is a cautionary tale of one such boy. Allow me to narrate.

A young boy lives in a far-off land. He hears stories of a beautiful palace and of the strong knights who joust on great horses. He longs to join the knights and battle with dragons. The boy borrows a bag of gold coins from a wealthy friend and promises to pay the friend back once he is doing well at the palace. He works hard and travels the country gaining work experience in whatever way he can. Having gained considerable experience and now feeling that he is finally ready, he goes to the palace and is put to a test. He passes the test and is welcomed to join the king's army. He is warned, however, that he must endure many years of training before he will be eligible to join the ranks of the great knights.

The boy's enthusiasm quickly falls away. Being in the king's army, he discovers, is not as glamorous as the stories had made it out to be and he must endure many more years before he can be considered for knighthood. The boy does indeed battle and kill dragons but he soon tires and decides that the palace is not for him after all.

He leaves the palace and decides to join the small army owned by a nobleman (the boutique law firm). The boy reasons that, having worked for the prestigious king's army, he will surely be appointed immediately to a higher rank in the nobleman's army. He also tells himself that he will be respected by his peers, who are likely to be in awe of him due to his prior appointment. In addition, having a smaller property, the nobleman's home is less likely to be under constant attack by dragons and therefore he looks forward to having a more peaceful life.

Upon arriving at the nobleman's house, the boy finds that he is now, in fact, part of a much smaller army consisting of only 10 men. To his disappointment, he finds that the atmosphere expounded is much less hierarchical than at the palace and that he is therefore not given any rank at all. The nobleman is kind and there are indeed fewer dragons. However, with only 10 men to fight the dragons, the boy is kept almost as busy as he was at the palace but is paid less in wages for his efforts. The boy grows disillusioned and thinks to himself, "did I beg, borrow and slog only to end up working at the house of an insignificant nobleman?"

The boy decides to move on. He has heard of a band of men who are new in the country. They are part of a contingent sent to protect a famous prince from a far-off land (the US firm). The prince is reputed to be a hard taskmaster but pays his men handsomely. The boy thinks to himself, "Perhaps I will join the prince. I will work for a few more years, earn enough to get myself a wife and then move to the country of the prince."

The boy joins the ranks of the prince's men. He is put to work immediately and works long hours. He is paid well but must go into battle frequently with no time left to go in search of a wife. The boy grows more disillusioned. "I am right back where I started," he thought. "I had given up the idea of becoming a knight and yet all these years have passed and I still feel overworked. I have enough money but no time to spend it and I am still no closer to finding myself a wife."

Moral of the story: The grass always looks greener on the other side but law firms are not that different to each other. Stories and rumours abound, but the reality is that if you want a very different life, chose a different career.

www.ingramcontent.com/pod-product-compliance
Lightning Source LLC
Chambersburg PA
CBHW030042100526
44590CB00011B/303